MOSES

AND THE PARTING OF THE RED SEA

Adapted by Tess Fries
Illustrated by Cheryl Mendenhall

bendon®

© 2017 Bendon, Inc. All rights reserved.
The BENDON name and logo are trademarks of
Bendon, Inc. Ashland, OH 44805.

As a baby, Moses was saved by an Egyptian princess. He grew up in Pharaoh's palace.

After killing one of Pharaoh's brutal soldiers while trying to help a slave, Moses fled to the land of Midian. There he married a shepherdess and took care of her father's sheep.

One day while Moses was watching the sheep . . .

. . . he saw a bush covered in flames—but it didn't burn up! God spoke to Moses from within the bush: "Moses! Moses!"

Moses replied, "Here I am."

"Do not come any closer," God said. "Take off your shoes—because you are standing on holy ground." Moses took off his shoes and hid his face because he was overwhelmed and afraid.

Then God said, "I have seen how my people are suffering in their slavery—and have come to rescue them. I am sending you to Pharaoh to tell him to let my people go."

Moses was afraid and said, "Lord, they will not believe me and I will not know what to say or how to say it!"

God told Moses, "Bring your brother Aaron with you to help you speak. I will be with you both."

So Moses took his wife and sons and journeyed back to Egypt.

Moses and Aaron stood before Pharaoh and said, "You must let God's people go so that they can worship Him—or He will send plagues on Egypt."

Pharaoh said, "I don't know your God. I will not let your people go."

So God turned all of the water in the land into blood. The fish died and there was no water to drink. Even the pitchers and pots in the homes held blood instead of water. But Pharaoh would not free the slaves.

Then God sent thousands and thousands of frogs. They filled the river and came into the houses. Frogs were on beds and in ovens and on tables. Frogs were everywhere! Pharaoh said to Moses, "Ask your God to take all of the frogs away, and then I will let your people go." But when the frogs were gone, Pharaoh still said, "No!"

God told Moses, "Have Aaron strike the ground with his rod." So Aaron did, and instantly the sand became millions of gnats! The gnats crawled over every animal, man, woman, and child. It was terrible!

Then Moses said to Pharaoh, "Let my people go."

And Pharaoh said, "No!"

So God sent swarms of flies into Pharaoh's house and the houses of his servants. Soon flies covered the entire land. Pharaoh told Moses, "I will let everyone go; just ask your God to take these flies away!"

But when the flies were gone, Pharaoh changed his mind and would not let the people go.

God sent sickness and sores, hail and locusts. Each time, Pharaoh begged Moses to ask God to take the new trouble away.

And each time Moses did, Pharaoh would still refuse to let the people go.

God told Moses to stretch his hand toward the sky. Darkness spread over Egypt! After three days, Pharaoh sent for Moses.

"Go, but your animals must stay in Egypt."

When Moses said, "Our animals must go with us to serve the Lord," Pharaoh did not let the people go.

God told Moses, "I will bring one more plague. After this, Pharaoh will let you go."

At midnight, God caused all of the firstborn sons to die. Moses instructed the Israelites to put the blood of a lamb on their doorways so that the Angel of Death would pass over their homes. Pharaoh's own son died. In his great sorrow, Pharaoh called for Moses and Aaron and said, "Leave Egypt. Take your people and animals and go."

For 430 years, the Israelites had been slaves in Egypt. Now they packed all that they had and left with their children, their herds, and flocks of animals to follow Moses out of Egypt. God guided them with a visible pillar of cloud by day and a pillar of fire by night. Soon, the Israelites came to the edge of the Red Sea.

When Pharaoh realized that the Israelites had fled, he changed his mind and said, "What have I done?"

Pharaoh and his army chased the Israelites. When the Israelites saw the Egyptians, they were terrified!

Then God told Moses, "Lift up your rod over the water." The Israelites watched as Moses followed God's instructions.

God rolled the sea back so the people could walk through on dry ground.

Once the Israelites were across the sea, God told Moses to stretch his hand over the sea. The waves fell upon Pharaoh's army, and they were all drowned. The Israelites were safe!

God wanted the Israelites to believe in Him and put their trust in Him. God wants us to believe in Him, too.

If we put our faith and trust in God, He will always be there to help us.

The waters were divided, and the Israelites went through the sea on dry ground, with a wall of water on their right and on their left.

EXODUS 14:22 (NIV)

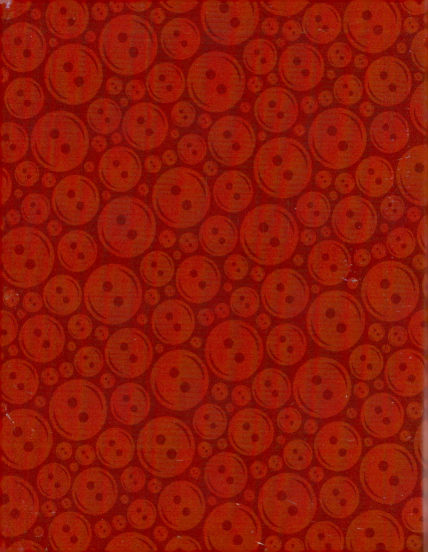